THE ROAD ONCE TRAVELLED

FRESH THOUGHTS ON CATHOLICISM

MARK GILBERT
WITH CECILY PATERSON

The Road Once Travelled

Matthias Media
(St Matthias Press Ltd ACN 067 558 365)
PO Box 225
Kingsford NSW 2032
Australia
Telephone: (02) 9663 1478; international: +61-2-9663-1478
Facsimile: (02) 9663 3265; international: +61-2-9663-3265
Email: info@matthiasmedia.com.au
Internet: www.matthiasmedia.com.au

Matthias Media (USA)
Telephone: 724 964 8152; international: +1-724-964-8152
Facsimile: 724 964 8166; international: +1-724-964-8166
Email: sales@matthiasmedia.com
Internet: www.matthiasmedia.com

ISBN 978 1 921441 87 5

Cover design and typesetting by Lankshear Design Pty Ltd.

CONTENTS

1 WE'RE IN THIS TOGETHER, AND WE KNOW WE'VE GOT ISSUES

Everyone is on a journey of faith. Everyone believes in something 'religious', whether it's God or Allah or the teachings of Buddha, or even just the idea that there is no God. And everyone is on a journey to work out what those beliefs mean for everyday life.

My journey as a Catholic began the very minute I was born.

My parents were committed Catholics, and so were their parents. Our family was a stable, comfortable suburban Catholic family. As kids, we went to Catholic schools, and our whole family went to Mass every Sunday. In fact, my parents made sure that church was the most important thing we did each week.

All of our big extended family events were also big church events: Christmas, Easter, weddings, funerals, my first Holy Communion and confirmation. Being Catholic was who we were. Even as kids we felt part of the Church. Once, when my six-year-old cousin saw his dad put five cents into the offering plate, he had something to say about it. The entire church laughed out loud when, from halfway down the pew, they heard a clear little voice ring out, "Five cents? Five lousy cents? They need more than that!"

I'm sure I wasn't the first Catholic kid to ask mum for money so I could go down to the front of the church to light a candle. That was what I told her, but what I really wanted to do was melt the wax and make sculptures.

I'm sure I wasn't the first altar boy to fall asleep up the front, or sneeze from the incense, or pick my nose when I thought no-one was looking.

And I know I wasn't the first Catholic kid to use my fingernail to etch words into the pews during Mass. Early on I figured out I could carve my sister's initials instead of mine so that she was the one who would get into trouble—not me!

I felt secure in our faith. I felt secure in our Catholic community. I knew all the priests and nuns from school, and I grew up with the kids from the church families. It was comfortable, it was always there, and it felt like nothing would ever change it.

The fact that we Catholics followed God also made me feel secure. I can't remember a time when I didn't know God and pray to him. Sometimes at school there were lunchtimes when things didn't go so well, and I remember the feelings of relief and peace when I sneaked into the church building to pray.

I felt secure in our faith. I felt secure in our Catholic community.

I also valued having ready access to a moral code to live by. In a world where so many issues were up for grabs, the stability of the Catholic Church's teaching on what's right and what's wrong helped a lot.

As I grew older, my faith took a more active turn. I felt I

could really make a difference in the world by doing good work. I got involved with raising money for charity, visiting homeless people and giving them food. I visited people in nursing homes, and helped run a drop-in centre for street kids. I even visited Indonesia with the St Vincent de Paul Society, to meet with some of the people we were supporting.

Everyone is on a journey of faith. You may be like me—Catholic from birth. Or you may have come to the Church later in life. But at some stage, you were out looking for a spiritual reason for being, for a way to make sense of this crazy life. And you began a journey that you hoped would help you do that.

But perhaps, like mine, your journey has stalled or been derailed. I got to a point at the age of about 17 where the Church seemed unable to give me answers to the questions I was asking. I felt frustrated. The road I was on didn't seem to be taking me in the direction I wanted to go.

Many people have similar experiences. Some might call it a 'crisis in faith'. Others just drift away. Take Elaine, for example:

> But it came to the point, I can remember clearly when it happened, that there was a Thursday that came up and I was planning to do something and then I remembered it was the Feast of the Assumption which was a Holy Day of Obligation and I had to go to Mass and I thought "I'm only doing this out a sense of obligation or duty". I thought if I'm doing it only for that reason, that's not a good enough reason. So that was the beginning of my falling off.[1]

As I go on in life, I meet people who are facing the same things I faced. People who are asking questions like these:

- Where am I going, and what is life all about?
- What is going to happen to the Church?
- What does the Church have to offer my children?
- Is it worth hanging in there?
- Is God just punishing me for something I've done wrong?
- Why do I feel so guilty all the time?

Simple statistics show that fewer and fewer people are finding their answers to these questions in the Church. In the 1950s, 60-65% of Catholics went to church on a given Sunday.[2] These days, only 14% of people who identify themselves as Catholics attend church on Sundays.[3]

Are you part of the 86% who don't? Perhaps you are looking for answers from the Church. Perhaps you have been holding onto frustrations that have irritated you for years. You may be like Helen, who says:

> It's my Church, yeah … I feel disenfranchised, I feel patronised, I feel alienated and I feel isolated. I feel distrustful and I feel angry [laughs]. Will that do for this morning? But I refuse to stop being a Catholic.[4]

Or perhaps you have given up faith and the journey entirely.

Whatever your story is, your questions and your frustrations are real, valuable and heartfelt. I can empathize with what you feel and think.

In fact, this book is actually really hard to write. While I want to be honest and clear about my disappointments and my questions, and the disappointments and questions of other people, I don't want to go on the attack.

There is an answer—a real answer—that has turned my life around.

The reason I'm writing it is not because I want to spend my time criticizing the Church. It's because I think there is an answer—a real answer—that has turned my life around and can certainly do the same for you.

And it's an answer that is right in front of all Catholics. As a seeker and fellow journeyer, I want to introduce you to that answer. His name is Jesus Christ. I met him through reading the Bible, and when I did that, my journey of faith took a whole new turn. In fact, I abandoned my own journey, and put my trust in *his* journey.

But before I get into that, I want to share some of the things I struggled with. You may be struggling with them too.

2 IRRELEVANT, BORING AND CONFUSING?

SOME PEOPLE GET SO INSPIRED BY THEIR FAVOURITE films that they dress up in costume and attend fan conventions where they listen to speakers, meet the original cast and mingle with other like-minded film fanatics. I've never been to anything like this, but I can imagine that if you were really keen about a film, it would be a great experience.

Just imagine, then, how you would feel if the main speaker at the convention was boring and dull or didn't know the film well. Imagine if he or she talked about issues that were unrelated to the film. Imagine if, all around you, film buffs started looking at their watches and shuffling their feet.

If this happened a number of times, the fans might start to lose their passion and move on to find a new favourite flick.

"It's lost its meaning", they might say. "It's not really what I thought it was."

If they really told the truth, they might come out with it. "I'm just bored. Where's the challenge? Where's the passion? Where's the film gone that I loved so much?"

While there were many things I valued about the Catholic Church as a child, Mass wasn't one of them. I found it excruciatingly boring. Being made to sit through prayers and responses recited one after another, week after week, was not my idea of fun. I can clearly remember thinking to myself at the age of seven, "When I grow up, I'm going to make this interesting!" I even planned a future career out for myself—I would apply to become the Pope so I could fix things up!

Every Catholic kid has a story about sitting in Mass—possibly involving paper pellets, scratching names into the pews, or hymnbook-paper origami. Many of us have stories about copping a belting afterwards because we wouldn't or couldn't sit still and listen.

Monica says:

> Words don't describe how boring Mass was growing up. All I know is your body goes into survival mode and you get the stares pretty bad. Daydreaming helped (especially about my current crush amongst the equally naughty and bored Catholic schoolboys). Anyway, I tried to pay attention but all the ups and downs and the genuflecting gave me a really sore right leg. So to wrap it up—it felt like what I think purgatory would be like—lots of waiting for it to end!
>
> Later in my life, I took my faith seriously and actually enjoyed a different church. I went back to my old Mass seven years later and didn't even realize that I had sat at exactly the same spot I always sat for all those years, and I must have been staring at the same crack in the church ceiling for at least ten minutes before I worked out what I was doing—I was on autopilot![5]

It would be great if we could say that now we have all grown up, we appreciate the services, the liturgies and the homilies.

But, sadly, more and more Catholics are finding they are unable to relate to what goes on in church. We just don't get it.

A recent research project asked some Catholics about their reasons for staying away from church.[6] Around half the people interviewed gave the irrelevance of the Church to modern life as the main reason, and only one of them didn't raise the issue at all. According to the final report on the research team's findings, participants thought the Church was out of touch with modern society. "In their eyes, the Church had lost its ability to connect with the day-to-day lives of ordinary people and as a result they no longer regarded it as having the authority to guide them in living an authentic life."[7]

There is a huge gap between what the Church teaches and what people who call themselves Catholics actually do.

Beverley is one of those people. She told the research panel, "the Church really lacks relevance … They've really lost touch with the reality of life".[8]

If being 'relevant' means scratching where people are itching, or recognizing the reality of people's lives, then perhaps the Church *is* irrelevant. Because the unfortunate fact is that there is a huge gap between what the Church teaches and what people who call themselves Catholics actually do.

The Church speaks against birth control, but is anyone in the pew listening? The birth rate amongst Catholics is the same as it is in the general population. I'm a father of three. Our children are wonderful, but my wife and I would find it hard to manage having more. We use contraception because we love the people already in our lives: each other, the kids, our family and our friends.

The Church speaks of divorce and remarriage as things that will exclude you from the Church, but who is listening? Every year, tens of thousands of Catholics get divorced and remarried.

The Church speaks and writes, but is anyone listening or reading? Nearly half the participants in the study I mentioned earlier also talked about the poor quality of homilies they had heard. They walked away from Mass every week feeling angry and frustrated.

The Church speaks, but is anyone listening with enough enthusiasm to actually put his hand up to be part of the leadership? For example, in 1997 not a single person was ordained as a Catholic priest where I live (in Australia). Numbers of priests are dropping, and the age of priests is increasing. The problem is often managed by importing priests from another country, many of whom struggle to understand the culture in which they suddenly find themselves.

The Church may be speaking, but if no-one is listening then it is, by definition, irrelevant. And as its teaching and actions become more and more separated from the world around it, it becomes more irrelevant. Sarah, for example, says:

> I started to think, "No, I can't cope with this any more. I can't believe all of these things that I am saying." I want to go along to a church service that is loving and spiritual and in tune and relevant and has words that mean something. Not a priest that stands up there and preaches at you that reads his service off the internet that says, "You do this, this and this or else".[9]

And Kathleen says:

> … it wasn't big things that made me leave in the first place, it was that living day to day, not having the tolerance to put up with, listening to what I believe nine times out of ten was drivel. I'm sorry but that's the way it came across to me.[10]

The number of disillusioned Catholics is large—and growing. And this is what they are saying. They feel bored. They feel that their church doesn't relate to them. And they feel confused.

Even though I went to Mass every week, I remember being confused myself as I tried to put all the teachings of the Catholic Church together.

I found the teachings on sex and marriage particularly confusing. For example, why was masturbation compared to murder? Why was skipping Mass as serious as cheating on your wife? (Both are mortal sins.) Why were priests not allowed to marry? And why were Catholics who married outside the Catholic Church excommunicated?

In fact, as I got older and thought more seriously, I found it harder and harder to hold it all together. So many parts didn't seem to make sense.

I was also confused by the way the teaching of the Church seemed to change. When I was growing up, for a while it was all fire and brimstone, but the next minute it was cool and easy. I can still remember the stir when the Catholic Church paid for advertisements on television that said, "When you get to heaven, what do you think he'll [God] say?" Answer: "He'll say g'day!"

I didn't get it. Was God strict and did he punish severely, or was he just a good bloke? And if God was so loving and powerful, then why did he let Jesus die that way?

The number of disillusioned Catholics is large—and growing. And this is what they are saying.

Leaders in the Catholic Church have done some things to try to change this. Vatican II was a massive attempt to make church more relevant to people in many parts of the world. Services were now conducted in the local language rather than in Latin, and more cultural elements were incorporated. The Church also began to address a number of the ethical issues facing the world at the time, like:

- What is human life?
- How can people from different cultures and religions understand each other?
- How can we make sense of rapid technological changes?

Another change has been the rise of World Youth days. I was involved in one of the first in Sydney, where we had 50,000 young people hanging out with the Pope. It was great fun. I was also part of the international World Youth Day hosted in Sydney in 2008, when up to 400,000 young people from around the world grooved through the centre of the city for a week. It felt great to see so many young people from around the world peacefully having a great time and talking about God!

But not long after the party is over, the boredom and the confusion and the feeling of irrelevancy returns. Is there an answer? Do we all just have to put up with it? Are we unspiritual and even sinful for feeling this way? Can anything ever change?

A little later in this book, I'm going to put to you that the answer to boredom, confusion and irrelevant religion is Jesus. But first, I want to talk about guilt, disillusionment and leadership.

3 | FEELING GUILTY YET?

MY SIX-YEAR-OLD SON, STEPHEN, LOVES TO COLLECT things. Most of the time his hobby is completely harmless, and great fun for him. Sometimes, however, he 'collects' things that aren't his and hides them in his bed. When we find them he gets really upset.

Why does he get upset? It's complicated. He knows he's done the wrong thing and is ashamed of what he's done, but at the same time he finds it hard not to take things, so he takes them and then feels guilty.

As his Dad, I've got a few options. It would be easy for me to just tell him he's done the wrong thing and punish him. It would also be easy for me to see how upset he is about it and not do anything at all.

But neither of these things helps Stephen deal with his guilt.

If I punish him, he feels worse about what he has done. If I let him off, he still knows he has done the wrong thing, and when he does it again, he will still feel guilty.

Guilt is a feeling I knew well in my childhood. As I tried to live out the Catholic life, I often became discouraged. There were so many rules. I knew all of them and I also knew how often I broke them.

I knew fighting with my sister was the wrong thing to do, but time and time again I would do things to provoke her and cause a fight. When I went to confession (which wasn't often), I would confess these things and be genuinely sorry. But that would last only a day or two before I was back to starting fights.

Some days I would do all right. If I tried really hard, I could last a few weeks without a fight, but then we'd be at it again.

Fighting with my sister seems a bit trivial, I know. But as I got older, there were other things I felt guilty about. For example, I looked at a lot of porn. This obviously isn't an easy thing to talk about (let alone put into print), but a lot of people struggle with the problem and we need to talk about it. I knew it was wrong, but I enjoyed it and I kept doing it. Occasionally I would confess my sin to a priest. He would tell me I was forgiven, give me some penance and tell me not to do it again. But within a few days I would.

I would resolve to change, and the guilt would subside for a while. But it never completely went away …

Sometimes I could go for a while without looking at porn—I remember once going for about three months without it—but then within a day I'd be back to my old patterns. Other times were much worse. I would do it and then feel guilty and bad and evil until I could get that great feeling of relief by going to confession and being pardoned by the priest. But it wasn't long until the next day, when it all began all over again.

The feeling of guilt for me was like the chicken pox virus.

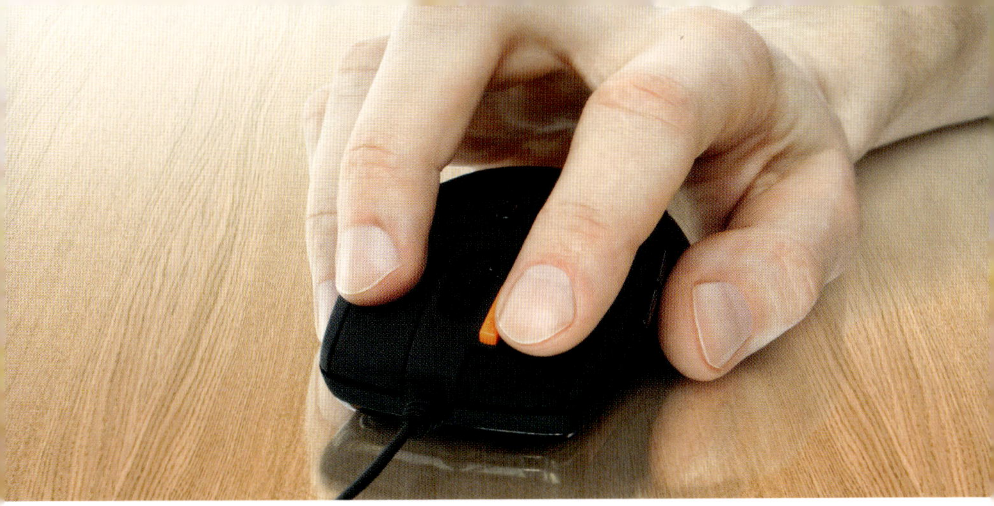

Once you've got it, you've always got it. It lives quietly in your body—usually imperceptibly, but ready to flare up when your defences are down.

As I got older, I noticed a pattern in my guilty feelings: they would cause a crisis in my life, drive me to prayer and action, subside for a while, and then return. My feelings of guilt would come to the surface particularly during church retreats and conferences, when I'd feel closer to God and more aware of how far short of his standards I was living. I would resolve to change, and the guilt would subside for a while. But it never completely went away, and I never made much progress on the things I felt guilty about.

For a while I tried to make myself feel *guiltier* about those things so that I might be motivated to do something about them, but when I couldn't see progress or improvement, it just seemed easier to stop caring.

In the end, it all seemed impossible. I fluctuated between feeling guilty for all the things I was doing wrong, and disregarding the rules all together and just doing whatever I wanted to.

Most Catholics will understand what I'm talking about. Guilt is a big issue for us. Several of the participants in the survey of ex-Mass attendees said that even after they had stopped going to Mass, they continued to feel guilty and were conscious of a fear of going to hell. In fact, they often said that these things prevented them from being able to trust in God and reach a more mature faith.

Occasionally guilt surfaces when things go wrong in life. "God must be punishing me because I'm guilty" is a common thing to hear. For example, Monica says:

> I had a really bad self-esteem issue, like I was a very bad person deep down for years and years, and I still struggle with people not accepting me or that God will smite me big-time. Also, I felt like I had to earn back his love, and other people's maybe—penance. Mind you, I wasn't the best example of a Catholic growing up either … I was a bit naughty.[11]

Guilt is always there. But it's not always at the surface. We frequently deny or suppress it, and sometimes it is blunted or dulled as a protection. We say to ourselves, "She'll be right mate—don't worry, switch off, don't think about it", because we don't want to face these guilty feelings that we can't do anything about.

We are all just like my son when he 'collects' things that don't belong to him. He hides his stolen treasures in his bed. We hide our failings behind whatever defences we can muster, and we feel guilty about them. The Church comes along and points out our sinfulness. We feel upset about it. We do our penance (punishment), but we know we're going to fail again and we know we can't stop sinning, so we wonder what the point is, and in the end we stop caring.

The Church's teaching about sin goes something like this:

1. You're basically a good person, but you have to obey God's rules.
2. There are a lot of rules for you to keep so that God will accept you.
3. It's pretty much impossible for you to keep the rules, so confess that you can't do it, take your punishment, and try harder.

Telling someone that something they do is sinful without helping them to change causes a whole lifetime of guilt and frustration. People get frustrated at the unreasonable expectations the Church places on them, and then feel guilty when they cannot meet these expectations. In the end, it's easier to leave the system than spend your life feeling bad about yourself.

So what do I say to my six-year-old in his upset state? He's done the wrong thing and he knows it. I could punish him or I could let it go, but neither option helps him with his guilt.

What I *do* is talk about Jesus, and the idea of grace.

Grace is the only answer I've found that deals with guilt effectively, and Jesus is the only one powerful enough to help us change our behaviour.

We'll get onto this more a bit later. But first, we need to look at another reason why so many Catholics are leaving the Church.

4 | WHO'S THE BOSS?

I'M A BIT OF AN ELECTION JUNKIE. VOTING CAMPAIGNS have it all—big personalities with big aspirations, power plays, promises, voting shocks and, of course, catchy slogans.

The Obama victory was like a feast for politics watchers. Here was a fresh face promising a new way forward. From the beginning, everyone had high hopes for him.

People hoped that he would be not only a great national leader but a careful and brilliant international diplomat as well. They wanted him to improve education, health, trade and defence. They wanted him to win the war, to withdraw from the war, and to close Guantanamo. African-Americans especially watched closely as 'their' Obama became the first African-American president to take office. And *everyone* wanted him to fix the economy.

These are the sorts of things we all hope for in our leaders. We want them to be fair, competent, strong, courageous and willing to fight for the most vulnerable in society. In some ways, that doesn't sound like too much to ask. But is there really anyone out there who can do *all* of that *all* of the time?

When politicians are popular, we have such high hopes for them. At the beginning of their time in office, we think they *can* do it. They can make the changes. They can fulfil our expectations and dreams. They can make life better for everyone.

But after they've had a few falls, told a few lies and hidden a few backdoor deals, we get disillusioned. Then we start looking for the next person who can fulfil our aspirations. Our leaders always fail and we are always disappointed.

This doesn't only happen with politicians. In any situation where we are looking to other people to lead us and show the way, disillusionment is just around the corner. Teachers, doctors, athletes, celebrities and musicians are all people we look up to as we find our way through life. They almost always disappoint us in some way or another. I know they are generally good sorts of people, and they all mostly try their best. It's just that they fail, at least sometimes —no matter who they are.

> *For various reasons, big or small, we get disillusioned with our leaders, priests, bishops and mentors at various times.*

Sadly, it's the same at church. For various reasons, big or small, we get disillusioned with our leaders, priests, bishops and mentors at various times.

The statistics are speaking for themselves. In the survey of people who didn't go to Mass any more, around 35% of them said that disillusionment with the Church leadership was the main reason they had left the Church.

Incompetence is a common reason for disillusionment. Sometimes the priest or the leader just isn't very good at the job.

But sometimes it's a bit more serious than that. The examples people gave included a priest who struggled with alcoholism, another who was having a relationship with a woman, and another who was out of touch with the outside world. One lady who is separated from her husband gives this as her reason for leaving:

> I was on my own with my kids, and he used to make comments about people who were divorced and all this stuff, it used to really break me, yeah, I just thought "This is somebody who's actually bothering to come to church" and he was there telling me, you know, "You're not doing the right thing", so that really annoyed me and there were lots of things that he said that I just didn't agree with.[12]

Incompetence is one thing. Power issues are another.

Many people are frustrated with what they see as an unequal sharing of power between the priests and bishops and the regular members of the Church. Some are unhappy about the fact that we raise the money, but we don't get to say how it's spent. Others don't like how the rules are made and enforced 'from above', as they say. If the Pope makes a ruling about faith and morals, it carries the authority of God. With a label like *papal infallibility* on what someone says, there might be room for discussion, but there's no room for dissent.

Quite honestly, there are times in my family life when I wouldn't mind having *fatherly infallibility*. My children ask a lot of questions, and sometimes they even point out when I've made the wrong decision. A little bit of infallibility might just control them and keep my 'glorious-father' status intact.

Fatherly infallibility might appear to be a good thing, if not for the whole family's peace and quiet, then at least for me. But in the end, it wouldn't be good for any of us. The children would lose their ability to think and question because they would be controlled. I might gain status and glory, but it would be a false glory. My children would not be giving their love and admiration freely, and my position would only exist as long as the control stayed tight enough.

> *There are times when I wouldn't mind having fatherly infallibility.*

Unfortunately, control and false status are the end results of a leadership system that is 'infallible'.

Some people in this world have great power—media barons,

CEOs of large and important companies, some politicians. But, at least in Western society, we all agree that power must be moderated with checks and balances.

To disillusioned or disagreeing Catholics, it seems unfair that the leaders of the Church have the power to excommunicate someone from the Church and the power to decide where a person will spend eternity.

The idea that the Church leadership has authority over the Bible also seems unfair to some Catholics. The Church teaches that it can be dangerous for Catholics to read the Bible for themselves.[13] I struggled with this issue myself. As a school student and then a medical student, I was encouraged to enquire and ask questions and find things out for myself, so it was disappointing to be given a hard time by the leadership of my own church for starting a Bible reading group.

Helen is someone who struggles with the way power is set up in the Church. She says:

> What would I like to see change? I'd like to see a decentralization of power, that's for a start. I would like to see the bishops allowed to fulfil the role that I think they are ordained to do. Which is teaching. My understanding is that the primary role of the bishops is to teach. And to pastor his people. When I said culture of arrogance I think that was an umbrella thing that pervades everything so that everything is seen through the prism of "We have all the knowledge, we have all the wisdom, we have all the power" so whether it's professional accountability, whether it's sex, whether it's structures, whether it's the pastoral dimension of the priesthood …"[14]

Susan feels angry about what she sees as a power grab by leaders. She says:

> I think the people in power have lost the humanness and it's about power. Sorry, I just think they are power mongers and they're just grappling their way up the ladder somehow and they are not looking at their general flock and being loving and caring. That, to me, that does make me angry because I think it's hypocritical.[15]

I think it's fair to say that some of the hardest things Catholics have had to face in recent years have been the sexual abuse scandals that have made headlines around the world.

The scale of these scandals is almost unbelievable. One study found that from 1950 to 2002, 10,667 people made an allegation of child sexual abuse against a total of 4,392 different priests in the US.[16] And although this was an American study, we know that similar things have happened all around the world.

It seems unfair that the leaders of the Church have the power to decide where a person will spend eternity.

Sadly, it won't end there. Many victims of abuse like this wait years or decades to report it—if in fact they report it at all. Based on the number of allegations made so far, the study estimated that at least 5% of all priests had an allegation of abuse made against them.[17]

The fact that these things have happened is a major source of disillusionment. The awful truth is that thousands of church leaders have instigated and taken part in serious crimes, usually directed against children and other vulnerable members of society. A second awful truth is that other church leaders have in many cases tried to cover up these abuses and, in some cases, protect the abusers.

As stories of abuse and mistreatment of vulnerable people have come out in the press, many Catholics have been so affected by them that they are leaving the Church.

In the survey of people who no longer attended Mass, 68% of the participants raised the misuse of authority and power at all levels of the Church as an issue. Sylvia, for example, says:

> I feel the Catholic Church is the most evil cult of all because of the paedophiles. And their abuse of the children in their care. And the cover-up by the hierarchy. Being betrayed by the Church you have attended all your life is the pits. You know, it's just removed so much from our lives … These men must not believe in God or they could not do what they do to children.[18]

So many Catholics are disillusioned with their leaders. We struggle with the idea that they can fail in big and little ways. It's just like the way we start out being so hopeful about our politicians and then get cynical when they fail, which they inevitably do.

Is the problem with us? Do we expect too much of our priests and ministers? Surely we can see that priests, bishops, nuns, brothers—hey, even the Pope—are just people like us, prone to failure and falling? Why should we be so extremely surprised when things go wrong?

On one level, I think we *do* expect too much—of *all* our leaders, whether they are spiritual or secular.

On another level, it is fair to say that the high expectations we have of priests are actually created by the Church. When someone becomes a priest, he is given an "indelible spiritual character".[19] It's different from any non-ordained Catholic. In fact, the whole system of pope, bishops and priests creates different levels of spirituality.

Unfortunately it seems that it's impossible for all the leaders, all the time, to live up to the exalted status they are saddled with. The reason is that they, too, are people. We are all imperfect, and we all struggle, whether we are ordained or not.

What is the answer? Is it to live with disillusionment and bitterness for the rest of our lives?

I want to tell you about Jesus, and how he deals with our disillusionment. But to do that, I'll have to start a new chapter.

5 WE'RE IN THIS TOGETHER, BUT WE'VE GOT JESUS

A FRIEND OF MINE WAS INVITED RECENTLY TO BE PART of a book club. She was new in town and wanted to get to know people, plus she loves reading and discussion, so she went along. She's not a Catholic, but she discovered that more than half of the women in the group were. Some went to Mass regularly while others didn't. A few said they had baptized their children so that their children could attend the local Catholic school.

One night the discussion took a turn away from the book they were reading, and a few of the women started to vent their dissatisfaction with the way church was going for them.

My friend didn't join in because she didn't attend the church, and she felt it would be rude to criticize someone else's religion. But when she heard one of the women say, "I just go, I sit up the back, I cringe all the way through it and then I get out of there as soon as I can", she was curious.

"If you feel that way about it, why do you go at all?" she asked.

"I'm Catholic!" the woman said, a little bit incredulously and fairly defensively. "It's our religion, so we can criticize it.

We might not like it, but at least it's ours."

In the survey of Catholics who didn't go to Mass any more, more than half said they still had faith even though they did not attend church. Most of these continued to call themselves Catholics. They still wanted Catholic baptisms, weddings and funerals. James says:

> In terms of global religions, I see myself as a Catholic. I see Catholic as a word which has many, many connotations [but] I'm exercising my responsibility as a thinking adult to be in communion with my God.[20]

In a way, I feel a bit the same. Whilst I've now left the Catholic Church, I still cherish my Catholic heritage and I identify with people having these struggles. I can relate to the woman in my friend's book club.

So far in this book I've talked a lot about the dissatisfaction, disillusionment and hurt that many of us experience in our journeys to God. I'm ready to start pointing to the answers, but one thing I want to be clear about is that we don't actually have to go anywhere different to find them. We Catholics have always had the answers. They are right at the heart of our faith, and they've been staring us in the face for generations.

The answers are right at the heart of our faith, and they've been staring us in the face for generations.

Some people are able to see them straight away, even though they don't like much of what their Catholicism gives them. Robert, for example, says:

> The million rules or something don't sort of suit me and this prescriptive stuff, the black and white doesn't suit me. The guidance about how we should relate to other people and lead our lives, that comes from Christ's teachings and I'm perfectly comfortable with that.[21]

Sarah can see it too. She says:

> And to me, Jesus loved people. He loved sinners. He comforted and embraced everybody and to me Jesus is a part of God … But Jesus who I love and who I talk to and pray to and believe in doesn't act like Bishop X and like a lot of those people who to me are just awful people …[22]

The answer to disillusionment with the hierarchy, the answer to seemingly irrelevant religious practices, the answer to ongoing feelings of guilt—all of these answers are found in Jesus.

And Jesus Christ should be at the centre of our faith.

Jesus is the perfect answer to boring, irrelevant religion

I think Jesus is the most fascinating person who ever lived. It's a big claim, I know, but here are some of the reasons.

Jesus' teachings have stood the test of time. He was the first to speak such classic pieces of wisdom as "Love your enemies", "Where your treasure is, there your heart will be also", and "First take the plank out of your own eye, and then you will see clearly to remove the speck from your brother's eye" (Matthew 5:44, 6:21, 7:5).[23] And there's plenty more of these in his teaching.

But Jesus is not just known for his teaching. He is also known for the extraordinary promises he made to ordinary people.

People ran to Jesus for help with all sorts of troubles, large and small. When a man whose daughter had just died came to Jesus, heartbroken and crying, Jesus promised that if he believed, his daughter would be made well (Luke 8:49-55). And she was.

Jesus promised that the least in this world will be the greatest, that those who mourn will be comforted, and that the meek will inherit the earth (Luke 9:48; Matthew 5:4, 5:5).

Jesus promised people an extraordinary life in this world, but more than that he promised people eternal life. How could he do this? Well, Jesus promised that he could fix our broken relationship with God.

It is our bad attitudes and behavior that keep us from God and make God angry with us. Jesus promised to make all that go away, giving us a perfect relationship with God.

"Take heart, son; your sins are forgiven", he said to a paralysed man who came to him for help (Matthew 9:2).

It's wise to be wary of people who make lots of promises. The truth is that most people can't deliver on the promises they make. However, Jesus not only made extraordinary promises; he also made amazing claims about himself. And if his claims are true, it means that he can keep every extraordinary promise he made.

What were his claims? Astoundingly, Jesus claimed to be a king who would live forever and sit at the right hand of God, ruling the universe.

These days, if someone claims to be God, or even a prophet, most of us agree that he or she is headed for the nuthouse or, at the very least, in need of some very strong medication.

Was Jesus suffering from similar God-delusions? Well, no, because—unlike every other person who thinks he is God—Jesus actually proved his claims by what he did.

I don't think I'm far off in claiming that Jesus was the most fascinating person who ever lived.

Jesus brought dead people back to life: the son of a widow, and a man named Lazarus (Luke 7:11-15; John 11:1-44). He cured a man born blind from birth—something that hasn't been done since, even in today's era of amazing medicine (John 9:1-7). Jesus walked on water, cured the paralysed, and fed thousands on a few loaves of bread and some fish (Matthew 14:25, 9:6-7; Luke 9:12-17).

Jesus did many other things too. But the most amazing thing he ever did was rise from the dead to rule with God forever.

I don't think I'm far off in claiming that Jesus was the most fascinating person who ever lived. He taught amazing things, made extraordinary promises, claimed to be God and to rule forever, and then proved these things by his actions.

But that's not all.

He did one more extraordinary thing. He called everyday sinners, like you and me, to be his followers. All we have to do is trust him and follow him.

Jesus invites us into an extraordinary relationship that affects every part of our lives. No longer are our lives boring, meaningless or irrelevant. The greatest man in history calls us to live our lives for him.

We can join with him in his struggles, share with him in his victories, and follow him into eternity with God. And if we are really following this fascinating, amazing person Jesus, we will never experience boring, irrelevant religion again!

Jesus is the answer to our desires for good, wise and strong leadership

When we think of Jesus, two images often spring to mind. First is Jesus as a baby: cute, but helpless in the manger. Second is Jesus on the cross: compassionate, but still ultimately helpless as he dies.

It's not often we see images of Jesus as a leader. But if he'd lived in the age of the internet, all the big buzz sites, popular YouTube clips and blogs would have been about him—because he was big, big news in AD 30.

People all over the place were leaving their homes and selling their possessions to come and follow Jesus. He had everybody talking, from the children to the leaders of the day. Powerful people held meetings to decide what they would 'do' about him.

He had a massive impact from one end of the country to the other.

Jesus was known for his teaching. Unlike the other leaders of the day, people said that Jesus taught "with authority", and thousands came to hear him (Mark 1:22, 27-28). He was known for his miracles, which were unbelievable and yet undeniable. He had the ability to answer his critics and yet he didn't try to win power or play political games.

He was busy. He knew what his plan and priority and mission were, yet he always had time for the little people: the children, the weak and the disenfranchised.

In only three years, Jesus went from being unknown to having a large following of ordinary people. And when the authorities thought they had seen the last of him after organizing his execution, they certainly didn't expect to hear about him again, let alone for a church to emerge that was strong and growing, passionate and vibrant, and which produced people who were willing to die for their faith in their leader, Jesus.

Jesus was a leader. That's what he was then, and that's what he still is now. Jesus is anything but helpless. His leadership is strong, tender, relevant and trustworthy.

Human leaders let us down; they always have, they always will. But Jesus won't. He asked his followers to give him their trust back then, and he asks us to give him our trust now.

And we *can* trust Jesus, because he has power over all things. Jesus has power to speak for God in the Bible (Luke 4:21, 32). Jesus has power over all the evil in this world (Luke 4:33-36). Jesus has power over all sickness and suffering in this world (Luke 4:38-39). Jesus has power over the forces of nature

(Luke 5:1-9). But most of all, Jesus has the power to make things right between God and us (Luke 5:17-26).

What's more, Jesus rules forever. On the rare occasions when we do get an extraordinary human leader, like Julius Caesar or Winston Churchill or Pope John Paul II, they only lead for a time. And throughout their leadership, there will be times when they lead effectively and times when they don't. Jesus doesn't have that problem because he leads forever. He is alive today and always in control, and he still speaks to us today through his word the Bible. He will never let us down, he will always be there and he will outlast us all.

Human leaders let us down; they always have, they always will. But Jesus won't.

Sure—there is still a place for earthly leaders in all sorts of areas, but once we follow Jesus directly, these other leaders become much less important.

Our search for a good and wise and strong leader is over. He is alive today and his name is Jesus.

Jesus is the answer to the problem of guilt

By dying on the cross, Jesus has paid for all the sins of everyone who trusts and follows him—and that means past, present and future sins. For anyone who isn't quite sure whether they will make the grade when Judgement Day comes, this is really good news.

Whether you have gone to confession or not, whether you have done penance or not, whether you go to Mass or not, there is no debt outstanding between you and God if you trust and follow Jesus (Romans 8:1).

What does this mean? It means that there is a way to be certain that you're going to heaven. It doesn't depend on how good you are. It depends on who you trust and follow. With Jesus, there's no more guilt and no more uncertainty.

Remember the story of Jesus talking to the criminals on the crosses dying next to him (Luke 23:32-43)? The first guy, who clearly doesn't trust or follow Jesus, mocks him: "Aren't you the Christ? Save yourself and us!"[24]

But Jesus didn't save himself, though he easily could have. He didn't save himself because he wanted to pay for the sins of his followers and save them. It's ironic, isn't it? By *not* saving himself, Jesus is saving the very people who are ridiculing him for not saving himself.

The second criminal gets it right. He says to the first guy, "Don't you fear God, since you are under the same sentence? We are punished justly, for we are getting what our deeds deserve. But this man has done nothing wrong."

The next thing he says shows that he believes and trusts Jesus: "Jesus, remember me when you come into your kingdom".

Jesus' response is instantaneous. He says, "I tell you the truth, today you will be with me in paradise". There's no confession needed and no penance to be done. Jesus simply gives complete eternal forgiveness. He can do this because he paid for the criminal's sins, just as he pays for the sins of anyone who trusts and follows him—whether they go to confession or not!

Now I can already hear you saying, "If Jesus has already done everything to forgive all my sins—past, present and future—then doesn't that mean I can sin all I like and still get to heaven?"

You're not the first person to ask that question. In the book of Romans, the apostle Paul asks the same question, concluding that following Jesus means leaving sin behind (Romans 6:1-14). This doesn't mean that people who follow him are never going to do anything wrong. Rather, it involves a change in outlook.

Before we trusted Jesus, we lived to please ourselves. Now, we live to please Jesus because of what he's done for us. We don't do it *so that* we can get to heaven, because Jesus has already done all that is necessary for us to get to heaven. Instead, because we realize sin is ultimately powerless over us, we are now free to live lives that are full, rich, beautiful, courageous and meaningful, all without getting stuck in the rut of guilt. Following Jesus gives us freedom from the burden of sin and its damaging effects, and freedom from guilt.

One spring holiday, I took my family to see the snow. Unfortunately the warm weather meant that the snow was already thick and wet. I carried a heavy pack for most of our trek up the mountain. It was thoroughly exhausting.

When we got near the top there was a steep slope of fresh deep snow. We took our backpacks off and bounded up the slope so we could leap, slide and tumble all the way down. It was fantastic. We couldn't stop laughing. The freedom we felt flying down the slope was amazing. And there was no way we were going to put our backpacks back on to climb another mountain.

The weight of sin in our lives is a bit like that heavy backpack on a long trek. The freedom Jesus brings is like the relief of finally taking it off. When I finally understood what Jesus had done for me, it changed my life!

Before, when I sinned, I thought my future was in jeopardy

and that I might end up in hell. In fact, I tried not to think about sin too much because it was too frightening.

But now, realizing that Jesus has done everything to pay for my sins—past, present and future—I have much more strength. I know that I am forgiven by God, even when I sin, because it doesn't depend on how good I am, or how hard I try, or whether I go to confession or not. It depends on what Jesus has already done by dying on the cross. When I sin now, rather than feeling guilty, I am grateful that God has done everything to save me.

Now that I have understood this, my relationship with God has gone from strength to strength. Paradoxically perhaps, freed from the guilt of sin, I've become better at not sinning. I still have a long way to go, but sin is no longer an unbearable burden.

Earlier I mentioned my son Stephen and his 'collecting' habit. Because Stephen trusts Jesus, when he does the wrong thing I can now say to him, "Jesus has already forgiven you for this. But you need Jesus' help to stop doing this, so ask him to help you not to take other people's things again."

Hopefully, instead of feeling guilty, Stephen trusts Jesus and is grateful that Jesus has forgiven him, and is strengthened not to do it again. He will probably do it again now and then, but he's on the right track.

If what I have just explained is news to you, then you might be asking, "Why haven't I heard this before?"

It is a good question to ask.

I found out about this good news when I was 17 and I started reading the Bible for myself and with other people. The Bible is full of this good news. It is better that you don't take my word for it, but find it for yourself in the Bible.

The idea that none of us can do anything to save ourselves, but that Jesus has done everything and all we need to do is trust and follow him, is found all throughout the Bible. That's a lot of reading to begin with, so if you want to see some specific, shorter examples then check out Luke 23:39-43, Luke 18:18-30, Ephesians 2:1-10, Romans 3:19-26 and Romans 8. In the Old Testament, you could read Psalm 22.

As I said at the beginning of this chapter, we're not going anywhere strange on our journey for answers. Jesus should be at the heart of our faith, and he turns out to be the answer to our disappointment with religion, our disillusionment with leadership, and our issues with guilt. We just need to follow him. And the best place to find him is in the Bible.

I still have a long way to go, but sin is no longer an unbearable burden.

But can the Bible really stand up to scrutiny? Can you really feel comfortable reading it for yourself? Could reading the Bible possibly change the way you see God, and the way you live life?

Come with me, and let me show you what I've found.

6 THE BIBLE—*THE* GUIDEBOOK FOR THE JOURNEY

My family likes hiking a lot. Well, perhaps I should be more truthful and say that I like hiking a lot, my wife likes it a bit, and the kids just come along.

I really like checking out new tracks when we travel to different places. One family holiday we were exploring a national park on the eastern coast of Australia. I knew there was an official track relatively close by but I wasn't sure exactly how to get to the beginning of it. Being the adventurous type, I said to my family with enthusiastic confidence, "Don't worry, the track goes along the coast. As long as we keep walking towards the coast we'll get to it pretty soon." We did get to the track, but it took 45 minutes of trying to avoid being scratched as we walked through thick scrub, and 45 minutes of listening to four worried voices saying, "Dad, are you sure this is right? Aren't we lost? Do you really think this is the way to go?"

If only I'd read the guidebook first, things would have been better. The guidebook mentioned the thick scrub. It had a map to show us how far off track we were, and it would have reassured my family when they were worried we were lost.

Guidebooks can keep us from making costly mistakes when we're travelling. If you don't read them, then like me, you can end up with a face full of scratches—or a lot worse! The more complicated a journey is, the more you need a guidebook.

But normal life is complicated too. Without a 'life guidebook', our journey here can quickly become a series of mistakes, sometimes with very painful consequences.

So where do we go to find wisdom and guidance in this world?

Many people go to their parents. I can think of some great things my parents taught me, like the importance of telling the truth and sticking at things even when they are tough. But my parents would be the first to say that neither they nor their wisdom are perfect.

Where do we go to find wisdom and guidance in this world?

Wisdom used to be passed down in traditions from generation to generation. However, times change. Most countries in the West have spent the past 50 years unravelling the traditions of the past and developing new ways to live. Traditionally, people went to the Church for wisdom, but like all other sources of wisdom, it has been found wanting. And the effects of misguided wisdom can be catastrophic.

Surely there must be a better way to navigate our way through this tricky world!

So far, I've put forward Jesus as the answer to our questions—and I mean Jesus as we find him in the Bible. The Bible is the best possible guidebook for our journey.

But aren't there just as many objections to the Bible as

there are to the Church? We could argue that hierarchy, guilt and irrelevance just come straight from the Bible. Isn't it out of date, unreliable and unreadable? Doesn't it just cause splits between churches?

I've been reading the Bible now for 20 years and, to be honest, I think these concerns are manufactured and overrated. In fact, I love the Bible. I've never read a better book. So I'll try my best to answer some of the biggest objections in the next few pages.

The Bible is boring, isn't it?

Do you get out to the movies much? You might have seen the Narnia series of films, or possibly *Star Wars, The Shawshank Redemption, Lord of the Rings, The Dark Knight* (Batman), *The Da Vinci Code, Moulin Rouge* and *Ice Age 2*—just to name a few that take their main plot or their morality or their inspiration from the Bible.

Seriously, the Bible is a blockbuster. It is *the* worldwide bestseller and the first book ever printed on the modern printing press. And it's been the basis for a whole other set of blockbusters—in film and literature—over the past few centuries. In fact, the Bible is full of great stories that have been told for hundreds of generations.

One common plotline in movies is the idea of one special, chosen person being able to save the world, and sacrificing himself to do it. Think *Die Hard*, the Harry Potter movies, *The Matrix* and *Star Wars Episode I* for starters. Those plotlines come straight from the Bible and the story of God's chosen son, Jesus, saving the world from sin through his death and resurrection.

It is true that people sometimes struggle with reading parts of the Bible. For example, the legal and technical sections in the book of Deuteronomy can be hard going. The long lists of family trees found in some of the Gospels seem dull to us. (African readers, however, who have a tradition of recounting their own ancestors, find these passages incredibly interesting!)

Because the Bible contains so many different types of writings, written for different purposes, some parts will appeal to some people more than others. There's poetry in the Psalms, stories told by Jesus in the Gospels, and practical wisdom taught by the apostles in their letters. And for some special people, the history or the legal sections in the Bible will be riveting.

I also think part of the problem people have in reading the Bible is breaking the barrier of getting into it. As with many of the best books, sometimes it takes a bit of time and effort to get the most out of it.

The Bible is the personal word of the God of the universe to you and me, so that we can know him clearly and live the way that's best.

Book clubs are popular again these days, and my book-club friend says that because of her group, she has read a number of books that she never would have picked up herself. Bible reading can be the same. Many people read the Bible in groups, sharing their knowledge and insights together. It's a great way to get extra understanding and motivation as you read.

So it might be interesting. But is it relevant?

The Bible contains the ideas on which our systems of government in the West have been built—the ideas of fairness, justice, accountability and the rights of individuals. The Bible was also foundational in the development of the English language. Even the word 'fisherman' was first penned in the Bible (Matthew 4:19).

But even more importantly, the Bible is the personal word of the God of the universe to you and me, so that we can know him clearly and live the way that's best. Because it is our creator who wrote the Bible (through human authors), it's even more relevant to our lives than the instruction booklet to the latest mobile phone you have bought.

The Bible is about the most important person who ever

lived: Jesus. It deals with the most serious problem humanity faces—sin—and it contains all the information necessary to receive eternal life.

Sometimes we get so caught up in our immediate lives—work, friends and family—that we lose sight of the bigger picture. No other book is as relevant to our past, our present and our future as the Bible.

I have found that after 20 years of regularly reading the Bible, God keeps showing me new and surprising things about himself, about his world and even about myself. I am yet to find a more useful and interesting book.

The Bible is for everyone—not just the experts

Some people steer away from the Bible because they think it is too complicated—a book for the experts. Or other people steer them away from it, saying, "It's dangerous! You might come up with the wrong interpretation."

I read the newspaper every day. I read books pretty regularly. Just like most other people, I learned to read at school, and I have a fair bit of experience in understanding what I read. If I took the attitude of worrying about getting the Bible wrong into the rest of my life, I would never read a newspaper or book by myself just in case I came up with the wrong meaning.

With a bit of care, the meaning of almost everything written in the Bible can be understood clearly.

The Bible is a book written by people who wanted to tell you something. When they wrote, they didn't think you would need an interpreter to understand them. They thought—just as the writer of any book does—that you would understand what they were saying by yourself.

God chose the Bible to communicate with people. If we can't understand the Bible for ourselves without an interpreter, then either God is a bad communicator, or the human race has become a lot more stupid over the past 2000 years.

Many of the books in the Bible are written by farmers and fishermen—not by scholars or philosophers. Jesus preached his parables to thousands of everyday mothers, fathers and children. He used everyday images that they and generations after them could relate to. He told stories about families, food, festivals, farms and friends.

God is perfectly capable of making himself clear without the aid of experts.

God is perfectly capable of making himself clear without the aid of experts. This is certainly what I and many hundreds of millions of others have found as we've read the Bible.

With a bit of time and effort we can understand the Bible for ourselves. In fact, understanding it is not the difficult part!

Jesus found himself in the Bible

Jesus himself took a keen interest in the Bible from an early age. He knew what we call the Old Testament very well. He understood what it meant and he was keen to explain it to others.

When Jesus was about 12, his parents lost him while the family was visiting Israel's capital city (Jerusalem) for a special religious holiday. His parents found him a couple of panicky days later—not hanging out with his mates playing first-century football, but sitting in the temple listening to the Bible teachers and asking them questions (Luke 2:41-46). Not the usual occupation of a teenager who has gone missing!

One reason the Old Testament interested Jesus so much was that he knew *he* was in there. His life's purpose and meaning was found in the Bible. He knew that he was the subject of prophecy after prophecy all the way through the Old Testament. The whole of the Bible was pointing to him as the special saviour that would come.

And he didn't keep this knowledge to himself. After he had risen from the dead, he spent time with his disciples explaining to them that the Bible was all about him. The Gospel of Luke records the fact that "beginning with Moses and all the Prophets, he explained to them what was said in all the Scriptures concerning himself" (Luke 24:27).

In fact, Jesus taught that everything written in the Bible about him must occur:

> "Everything must be fulfilled that is written about me in the Law of Moses,[25] the Prophets and the Psalms." (Luke 24:44)

Jesus also considered the Bible to be utterly reliable because the words of the Bible come from God. In the Gospel of John, he says, "the Scripture cannot be broken" (John 10:35).

Jesus expected everyone else to read the Bible too

Not only did Jesus stake his life on what the Bible said, he also expected everyone else to do the same. He expected people he met to know what the Bible said and to live by its teachings.

When a man asked Jesus how to get to heaven, Jesus didn't reply with, "What do you think?" or "What does the Church teach?" Instead, Jesus' question was, "What is written in the Law?" (Luke 10:25-26). And he expected the man to know.

In another example, Jesus told a story about a rich man and a beggar. Both men die, and the beggar goes to heaven while the rich man goes to hell. When the rich man realizes what has happened to him, he pleads with Abraham in heaven to send someone back from the dead to warn his family.

The answer is a big no. Abraham tells the rich man,

> "If they do not listen to Moses and the Prophets, they will not be convinced even if someone rises from the dead." (Luke 16:31)

In other words, Jesus is saying that if people have the Bible but don't listen to it, then they won't listen to anything else.

Is the Bible as good as an experience?

We all really want to be close to God. We want to touch God, to feel his presence, to experience him, to make him real in our lives. Religious experiences can do this for us—experiences like Holy Communion, prayer meetings, big rallies, retreats, and even listening to powerful talks.

At the same time, though, these experiences can leave us unsatisfied, wanting more, and searching out the next religious experience. They promise so much but fail to satisfy.

Again, Jesus has something to say about this.

I told you the story of how he got separated from his parents at the religious festival at the age of 12. What was the attraction that made him stay in the temple? It was not the festival itself. His parents searched the city for him and didn't find him. The attraction for Jesus was the activity of learning from and teaching the Scriptures. The Gospel writer puts it like this,

> After three days [his parents] found him in the temple courts, sitting among the teachers, listening to them and asking them questions. Everyone who heard him was amazed at his understanding and his answers. (Luke 2:46-47)

I've had my share of looking for religious experiences at camps, rallies and retreats, and even at regular weekly Mass. Yet in the end those experiences have often let me down.

The Bible isn't like that. Unlike some religious experiences that end up being vague and uncertain, the Bible is clear. You can be certain of what God says, what he means and what you need to do about it.

You can be certain of what God says, what he means and what you need to do about it.

The Bible is relevant, interesting and compelling. It never stops surprising, teaching and guiding. It is reliable and true.

The Bible brings me closer to God because I can actually hear him speak through it. By listening to him, I get to know him better.

The Bible helps me in my marriage, in raising my children and in my work life. It helps me manage my money and sort out my priorities in life. It is the one source of wisdom I can rely on completely in an uncertain and changing world.

In short, reading and understanding the Bible is the one religious experience I've had that actually works and keeps on working.

I've learned my lesson from my hiking experience. These days I know better than to set out on a difficult or dangerous walk without preparation, especially when I have my children in tow. I read the guidebook if I'm attempting something like that. It's the same in life. We need guidance. And we have a guidebook—the Bible—that is effective, reliable and relevant.

Doesn't the Bible cause factions and splits?

Another objection I sometimes hear is that reading the Bible leads to factions, disunity, and even church splits. To maintain unity, the solution (apparently) is that we need one authority to tell everyone else what the Bible means.

Let's just think about this for a moment. God used the authors of the Bible to write down what he wants to say to us directly. Peter, one of the early church leaders, writes this:

> Above all, you must understand that no prophecy of Scripture came about by the prophet's own interpretation. For prophecy never had its origin in the will of man, but men spoke from God as they were carried along by the Holy Spirit. (2 Peter 1:20-21)

In the end, God wrote the Bible. The Bible *is* the authority because God wrote it. If you believe this, then you have unity with everybody else who trusts the Bible, because you all trust the same thing.

You only get division when you add a second authority that

claims to interpret the Bible, because now there is the authority of the Bible *and* the authority of the person or people who interpret it. By adding an additional authority to the Bible, you create disunity.

I am happy to accept the authority of the Bible. I am also sceptical of the idea that any human or group of humans can always understand all of it perfectly.

Instead, why don't we say, "We can trust the Bible, but as far as humans go, we do our best to understand what God means, and sometimes we get it wrong"? Then at least we're willing to be corrected by the Bible when we're wrong.

Isn't the Bible too old to matter today?

How is it possible for a book written 2000 years ago to be more relevant to my life than something written today? Surely we need something more than a 2000-year-old book to go by?

Following Jesus' example helps us with this question too.

When Jesus was born, three quarters of the Bible had already been written. The Old Testament was already between 400 and 1600 years old. All that remained to come was the New Testament, which was written soon after Jesus died.

How is it possible for a book written 2000 years ago to be more relevant to my life than something written today?

While Jesus lived, he had a choice. When it came to living his life, he could have followed the teachings of the church leaders of the day or he could have followed the much older Scriptures.

As I said before, Jesus trusted the Scriptures as God's words

and *the* guide for his life, even though they were hundreds of years old.

In fact, Jesus often used the Scriptures to show the religious leaders where they were wrong. An example of this is when he is talking about the subject of resurrection with some Jewish leaders. Jesus says, "Have you not read what God said to you?" (Matthew 22:31) and then quotes Exodus 3:6, written about 1600 years earlier.

This is pretty amazing if you think about it. Not only did Jesus trust the Bible more than he trusted the religious authorities of the day, but he also thought that something written thousands of years earlier was written directly to people living in his day.

Jesus can say this because God doesn't change and people don't either. We all still sin and our greatest need is to be forgiven by God, whether we live in 1000 BC or 2000 AD.

The reason we can trust the Bible as our guide, even 2000 years after it was written, is that it comes from God and is perfect. Human institutions and authorities, on the other hand, are not always reliable.

Again, it all comes down to trust. Do you take your lead from Jesus and trust God as he speaks to us in the Bible? Or do you trust human institutions?

Please don't trust me. Check out the Bible for yourself, or join up with a group of people and check it out together.

7 | SO WHAT HAPPENS NOW?

OK, IT'S TIME FOR ACTION. TIME TO START READING the Bible for yourself. But how do you get started? Here are a few things that helped me when I started out reading the Bible for myself.

Start simple. Begin with one of the Gospels—the biographies of Jesus' life, written by some of his closest followers. Luke is a really good one to start with, and so is Mark.[26] It's short and full of action.

Read it *as a book*. This may sound obvious. But some people read the Bible differently from the way they read other books. Sometimes they take strange and mysterious meanings out of it that were never intended by the person writing the book. We are all used to reading, so just read it. Try to work out what point the author is making and how his ideas link together. The simpler the explanation, the more likely it's correct. You might find it helps to have a pen and paper to write down what you're learning and any questions you have.

Listen to it. The Bible is available in a number of different formats. There are kids Bibles with pictures, as well as plenty of well-produced audio books. The Bible is read aloud in churches every day of the week and taught in many different languages and styles. Anyway, Jesus' emphasis was always on listening!

Get a bit of background. Sometimes it can be helpful to know a bit about the culture at the time a particular book in the Bible was written. Sometimes the publisher of a Bible translation provides an introductory paragraph at the beginning of each book of the Bible to give you a bit of helpful background.

Get some resources. As I've jumped into the Bible, I have found John Dickson's book *Simply Christianity* to be very helpful.[27] Most Christian bookshops should have it or be able to get it for you. Alternatively, you can get it direct from the publisher.

Do something about it. Reading the Bible isn't just an intellectual exercise. God expects that as we get to know him better, our lives will change. So act on what you learn.

Find a group. It helps to read the Bible with someone else, or with a group of people who have been learning from the Bible for a number of years. I suggest you find people who believe that the Bible is God's first and last word—who trust it above all other wisdom. They are likely to be the most helpful to you. If you can't find a group, look online for a virtual community that reads the Bible.

Ask your questions. Don't be afraid to ask questions of the Bible. And you should expect to find answers. God can stand up to your scrutiny, and he wants you to find out more about him.

Just do it! No excuses—just get started. Don't just take my word for it—find out for yourself.

I STARTED THIS BOOK by describing my 'journey to God'.

I faced a number of obstacles, like my frustration with boring and irrelevant religious practices, and my desire for good, wise and powerful leadership. I struggled with guilt and being unsure about whether the good things I did were enough and whether the sins I kept committing were really forgiven. I experienced frustration with the fact that trying harder wasn't enough. I was just not making it.

As I started to read the Bible for myself, I discovered that someone else had also made a journey. But it was not just a journey to God. Jesus' journey was *from* God to us, and back again. He stepped down from his throne in heaven because he wanted to save us. He became a human and lived on the earth, just like us. He faced temptations, pain and hardship. He shared our journey.

But there is one very big difference between Jesus and us. Jesus made it.

Jesus lived the perfect life that we cannot live. Then he died on the cross to pay the price for our sin, and he rose from the dead to journey back to God and sit at his right hand in heaven (Mark 16:19). Jesus' actions achieved what our good works can never achieve—the forgiveness of our sins.

That understanding—that Jesus had already done everything to pay for my sin, that he'd made the journey I could not make—changed my life.

It was like the difference between dating someone and being married. When I thought it was up to me to deal with my sin, it was a bit like just dating God. I kept having to ask,

"Does he love me or doesn't he?" And I was never quite sure of the answer, especially just after I'd done something wrong.

When I understood that all my sins had already been dealt with—past, present and future sins—it was like being married. I finally knew where I stood with God: forgiven.

I also discovered that because Jesus had made the journey back to God on my behalf, I could follow him into eternity (1 Corinthians 15:20-23). In fact, because Jesus had already made the journey to God for me, I didn't have to. I could rest at last, trusting him and what he had done for me. For the first time in my life, I became certain of where I was spending eternity.

As I said, my life changed from that point.

I started reading the Bible regularly—not because I thought I should, but because I wanted to know more about this guy who saved me. I wanted to get to know *him*.

Two things happened as a result. First, the world made so much more sense to me. For the first time, I began to understand people, good and evil, and the answers to the big questions of life.

Second, I started to get rid of the ugly things in my life because I wanted to live a life that honoured Jesus. It's an ongoing and lifelong process, but I want to do it—whatever the cost—because of what Jesus has done for me.

Speaking of costs, I can't deny that there have been a few since I began following Jesus.

It was hard to have my family question my new-found commitment to Jesus, even though they were committed

Catholics themselves. It was also hard to take a different path from my friends. Changing my life cost me a few relationships.

However, I gained some even better relationships—great friends who have shared the good times and the hard times of following Jesus, and stood the test of time.

I can say from my own personal experience that Jesus' promise in Luke 18 is reliable:

> "I tell you the truth … no-one who has left home or wife or brothers or parents or children for the sake of the kingdom of God will fail to receive many times as much in this age and, in the age to come, eternal life." (Luke 18:29-30)

My life has taken a number of turns since that time. I spent many years active in the Catholic Church, leading Bible studies and working for the St Vincent de Paul Society, but in the end it seemed best for me to leave and join the Anglican Church, where I now serve as a minister.[28]

I don't know where your life will lead from here, but I hope and pray that you will find rest from your religious searching. I hope you'll find that rest in Jesus and what he has done. I hope that you will trust him, that you will know that he has indeed dealt with your sins, and that you will follow him as the good, wise and all-powerful ruler of your life. I hope that you will know him clearly by learning everything you can from the Bible.

Everyone's journey is different and, in many ways, is not that important—because the journey that really matters is the one that was made 2000 years ago by Jesus Christ.

The road only had to be travelled once. And Jesus travelled it. Now I can trust and follow him, knowing that he will get me to heaven. I hope you will too.

God bless you.

ENDNOTES

1 Robert Dixon et al., *Research Project on Catholics who have Stopped Attending Mass: Final Report February 2007*, Australian Catholic Bishops Conference Pastoral Projects Office, Fitzroy, 2007, p. 39. Available online, viewed 12 August 2010: http://www.ppo.catholic.org.au/researcharts/researcharts.shtml#movingAway

2 Michael Gilchrist, 'Catholic beliefs and practices: the challenge ahead for Australia', *AD2000*, vol. 18, no. 4, May 2005, p. 7. Available online, viewed 12 August 2010: www.ad2000.com.au/articles/2005/may2005p7_1927.html

3 The Australian Catholic Bishops Conference Pastoral Projects Office, *Frequently Asked Questions*, Pastoral Projects Office, 2005-2008, viewed 12 August 2010: www. ppo.catholic.org.au/faq/faq.shtml

4 Dixon et al., p. 44.

5 M Markovina, interview with Cecily Paterson, September 2009.

6 Robert Dixon et al.

7 Dixon et al., p. 18.

8 Dixon et al., p. 18.

9 Dixon et al., p. 18.

10 Dixon et al., p. 29.

11 M Markovina, interview with Cecily Paterson, September 2009.

12 Dixon et al., p. 27.

13 For example: "'The task of giving an authentic interpretation of the Word of God, whether in its written form or in the form of Tradition, has been entrusted to the living teaching office of the Church alone. Its authority in this matter is exercised in the name of Jesus Christ.' This means that the task of interpretation has been entrusted to the bishops in communion with the successor of Peter, the Bishop of Rome", *Catechism of the Catholic Church*, part 1, section 1, chapter 2, article 2, part III, 1993, paragraph 85. Available online, viewed 30 August 2010: www.vatican.va/archive/ENG0015/_ _PM.HTM

14 Dixon et al., p. 23.

15 Dixon et al., p. 23.

16 GW Lynch et al., *The Nature and Scope of the Problem of Sexual Abuse of Minors by Catholic Priests and Deacons in the United States: A research study conducted by the John Jay College of Criminal Justice*, United States Conference of Catholic Bishops, Washington DC, 2004, pp. 7 and 26. Available online, viewed 30 August 2010: http://www.usccb.org/nrb/johnjaystudy/

17 GW Lynch et al., p. 29.

18 Dixon et al., p. 23.

19 *Catechism of the Catholic Church*, part 2, section 2, chapter 3, article 6, part VII, paragraph 1582. Available online, viewed 30 August 2010: www.vatican.va/archive/ENG0015/__P4Y.HTM

20 Dixon et al., p. 44.

21 Dixon et al., p. 23.

22 Dixon et al., p. 23.

23 The way you can easily find things I'm referring to in the Bible is to use the references I give. First the name of the book is mentioned—for example, 'Matthew'; secondly the chapter number is given—in this first case, chapter 5; and thirdly the sentence number is given—this time, number 44.

24 The word 'Christ' refers to God's promised king, who will rule forever.

25 The Jewish people divided the Old Testament into three parts: the Law of Moses, the Prophets and the Wisdom books or Psalms. This verse is claiming that everything written about Jesus in every part of the Bible is true.

26 If you don't have a Bible, you can read it online. The New International Version is easy to read, and you can find it here: www.Biblica.com/bible/verse/?q=Luke1&niv=yes

27 Published by Matthias Media: www.matthiasmedia.com/rd.html?sku=scb

28 If you want to understand why I made this decision, I recommend that you read *Nothing in My Hand I Bring* by Ray Galea. He very clearly explains why he made the same choice as me. This book is also published by Matthias Media: www.matthiasmedia.com/rd.html?sku=nimh

Matthias Media is an independent Christian publishing company based in Sydney, Australia. To browse our online catalogue, access samples and free downloads, and find more information about our resources, visit our website:

www.matthiasmedia.com.au

How to buy our resources

1. Direct from us over the internet:
   - in the US: www.matthiasmedia.com
   - in Australia and the rest of the world: www.matthiasmedia.com.au
2. Direct from us by phone:
   - in the US: 1 866 407 4530
   - in Australia: 1800 814 360 (Sydney: 9663 1478)
   - international: +61-2-9663-1478
3. Through a range of outlets in various parts of the world. Visit **www.matthiasmedia.com.au/information/contact-us** for details about recommended retailers in your part of the world, including www.thegoodbook.co.uk in the United Kingdom.
4. Trade enquiries can be addressed to:
   - in the US and Canada: sales@matthiasmedia.com
   - in Australia and the rest of the world: sales@matthiasmedia.com.au